Fish-it4

Published by:
Arc Publishing and Print
166 Knowle Lane
Sheffield S11 9SJ

Produced By: Chris Keeling

Whilst every effort has been made to ensure the contents of this
publication are accurate at the time of publishing.
Arc Publishing and Print and those involved in producing the content
of "Fish-It 4 West Yorkshire" cannot be held responsible for any
errors, omissions or changes in the details of this guide or for the
consequences of any reliance on the information provided in it. We
have tried to ensure accuracy in this guide but things do change and
we would be grateful if readers could advise us of any inaccuracies
they have found.

ISBN: 978-1-906722-05-0

ACKNOWLEDGEMENTS
I would like to thank the following for there
help in producing this guide:
Bradford No1 Angling Association.
Jim Steele for venue information.

All fishery owners and angling clubs who have kindly
provided information and to those that gave permission to
use images from their websites.

Arc Publishing and Print
166 Knowle Lane
Sheffield
S11 9SJ

C O N T E N T S

W E L C O M E

Welcome to Fish-it 4 (West Yorkshire). As in my three previous books, I have tried to provide a mixed selection of venues to entice you to try a new fishery.

I hope I have produced a book that gives a good idea of what a fishing venue has to offer before setting out on a lengthy journey, only to be disappointed when you reach your destination.

There is plenty of information, along with photos of most venues, so hopefully you will find the ideal water to suit your method of fishing.

I have enjoyed fishing many of these fisheries, but not all. Information has been supplied to me from anglers and fishery owners from the area and I would like to thank them for their support.

If you have details of a venue and you would like it included in a future publication, please fill in the form at the back of this guide.

Hopefully you will find Fish-it 4 a useful guide in finding different places to fish.

Chris Keeling

I have tried to ensure the accuracy of this guide but things do change very quickly so if you know of any inaccuracies or any fisheries I have not included I would be grateful if you could fill out and return the form at the back of the guide.

GETTING STARTED

Fishing is enjoyed by many people as both a sport and a hobby. Basically anglers can be divided into three types. Firstly the pleasure angler who fishes just for the relaxation and fun - enjoying their surroundings but unworried about the number of fish caught (as long as they get a few).

The match angler is competitive and has a wide knowledge of the sport. He enjoys competing against other anglers and has an impressive collection of tackle which enables him to fish large lakes, small ponds, canals and rivers.

The specimen angler or hunter is a loner, usually intent on catching a large fish. Most specialise in a particular species - eg. carp, pike, barbel.

The specimen carp hunter can spend thousands on his tackle and many hours making special rigs in his bid to catch that really big fish.

Most people, however, take up fishing purely for pleasure.

To get started you will need the following:-

Rod: Most beginners start with a match rod. A good choice would be a 12' carbon fibre rod. Your local tackle shop will advise you, ask the assistant to fit a reel to the rod. It should be comfortable to hold and feel well balanced. Carbon composite rods are cheaper than the carbon rods. In the long run it pays to get a good carbon rod.

Reel: There is a wide range of reels. Again ask for advice from the tackle shop or try one of the many angling forums on the internet. You will get sound advice from more experienced anglers. Begin with a fixed spool reel which will cost you between £15 and £25. Most fixed reels come with two spools. Put 3lb line on one and a heavier line (6lb) on the other for catching larger fish.

Keepnet: Ideal if you like to see your catch when you've finished fishing. Make sure you get a large net and fully open it whilst in the water - this allows the fish room to move. Make sure it is at least 8' in length. They are made in either round or rectangular shape. Some have adjustable legs for use on sloping banks. Note, many fisheries don't allow keepnets except in matches. Check fishery rules.

Landing Net: This is a vital piece of equipment for landing a hooked fish. Again there are various sizes available. Don't buy one to small or you will have a problem landing that unexpected big carp! Never attempt to swing fish to hand, get into the habit of landing all fish no matter how small. Swinging in larger fish will damage the fish and could also break your rod.

Floats: There are many types of float to chose from, but wagglers are the most popular. The best way to attach them to your line is by fixing a float adaptor, this is a piece of silicon tubing with a swivel eye, which allows the float to be changed without breaking down the rest of your tackle. Most floats are made of plastic, balsa or peacock quill. For faster flowing waters many anglers use stick floats.

Seatbox: This is useful, not only as a seat but as a storage place for your fishing gear. The Shakespeare seatbox is very popular. It is made of light weight plastic with good storage space and two detachable trays - ideal for the beginner. More expensive boxes have hinged lids and separate storage compartments for rigs, plus adjustable legs for use on uneven ground.

Line: The line is a thin string made from a single fibre, this is called monofilament line. It comes in different colours but clear is the commonly used type. Monofilament degrades with time and can weaken when exposed to heat and sunlight. When stored on a spool for a long time, it may come off the fishing reel in coils or loops. It is advisable to change monofilament line at regular intervals to prevent degradation. Load your reel with 3 to 4lb line for float fishing. If you targeting heavier fish then use 6 to 8lb line.

Hooks: There is an enormous variety of fish hooks that will be on display at your local tackle shop. Buy hooks that are already tied to a nylon hook length and make sure you get barbless ones as they are much easier to remove from the fish. Size 22 (small) are ideal for small roach and perch, upto size 14 for larger fish.

Rodrests: These attach to a bankstick which is a pointed metal stick with a universal threaded end. There are many types of rests, just chose one that will support your rod comfortably.

Shot: Shot comes in sizes SSG to No8 and can be bought separately or in multi-size shot dispensers. The bigger shot is used to fix your waggler at the correct depth position on your line. The lighter smaller shot is used to sink your line and set the appearance of your float on the water surface.

Plummet: A plummet is a weight which is used to accurately measure the depth of water you are going to fish. They are attached to your hook. If the float disappears after you have cast in, then you are set too shallow and need to move your float up the line.

Disgorger: This is used to safely remove the hook from the mouth of a fish. The plastic barrel type are best. Simply slide the disgorger down the line until contact is made with the hook bend. Give it a slight push and out will come the hook.

Fishing Licence: Anyone over the age of 12 will need an Environment Agency Rod Licence. This allows you to fish for coarse fish but you will also require permission from the owner of the fishing rights. You can get this either by club membership or by purchasing a day ticket. Rod licences run for twelve months beginning on 31st March. Eight day and one day licences are also available. You can these from post offices or on line @ environment-agency.gov.uk/fish.
Adult licences cost £25.00 for a full year.
8 day licences are £9.00
1 day licences are £3.50
Junior (12-16 years) are only £5.00
There are also concessionary licences for people aged 65 or over.
(Check the Environment Agency web site for the latest prices)

In the cooler months you will need warm and waterproof clothing. An umbrella is also a good idea - get one that tilts. There are a few rules to keep everyone happy. Close all gates. Have respect for the landowner who has given permission for you to use his land and most importantly don't leave litter - especially discarded line and hooks.

Good fishing!

POLE FISHING
FOR THE BEGINNER

Of all the different methods of fishing I've tried, I haven't found any of them as accurate or as easy as pole fishing. To be able to place your bait and feed to the exact spot, sometimes only inches from an island or group of reeds is what makes pole fishing so productive and fun.

TACKLE NEEDED

A Pole

Poles come in various sizes, from 4 metres (usually called a whip) to poles of 18.5 metres. They also vary dramatically in price as well, this is usually governed by weight and rigidity. The lighter and straighter (no droop at the end) the more expensive they are. I recommend a pole between 11 and 13 metres, stay away from the smaller telescopic ones. Many tackle shops have poles ready assembled for you to handle, make sure you are comfortable with its weight and it feels well balanced. Test that it takes apart smoothly. If possible, get a pole with a spare top section as they enable you to rig up for different species and size of fish.

Pole Rigs

Experienced anglers can make up their own pole rigs but beginners are advised to buy ready-made. There are plenty of quality ready made rigs available for as little as £2.99. These rigs come with a main line with a loop on the end (used to attach the line to the stonfo connector at the tip of your pole). A float with enough shot below it to cock it nicely in the water and a length of lower breaking strain line, which has a spade end hook tied to it. The float and shot can slide down the line and be adjusted accordingly.

Pole Elastic

The elastic that runs through the top sections of your pole cushions the fight of a hooked fish and allows you to play it. Elastics are graded in sizes 1-20.
The following list is a good guide for the beginner:
1. For small roach and perch for example - use a No4 elastic with a 1lb hook length and a 2lb main line.
2. If fishing for small carp and tench or skimmer bream use a No8 or 10 elastic with a 3.5lb main line and 2.5lb hook length.
3. When fishing for carp up to 12lbs use a No16 to 18 elastic, and a main line of 8lb with a 6.5lb hook length.

START TO FISH

Fishing Position

Get your seatbox in position. Ideally, when sitting on the box, your thighs should be in a horizontal position, at right angles to your lower leg. Holding the pole correctly makes it comfortable for long periods and prevents backache. For a right handed person you need to rest the pole across your knees with your left hand supporting it. Put your right forearm along the end of the pole and firmly grip the pole with your right hand. Have close to hand - your bait, landing net, disgorger and anything else you may require for your days fishing. It is important to have your pole roller in the correct location. The pole has to be well balanced in your hands when it leaves the roller - this prevents rig tangles when shipping out.

Start Fishing

You have set up your pole and plumbed your depth - so now you are ready to fish. Make sure you have between 10" and 20" of line between the tip and float. In more windy conditions you may want to lengthen this. Feed your swim with groundbait (if allowed) plus a few bits of your hook bait. This is more accurately done using a pole cup which can be fixed to the end of your pole. Put your bait on the hook and ship out your pole trying to keep your rig in the water as this prevents tangles. Lay the rig on the water lengthways. The shot on the line will pull the line under the water and cock the float.
Enjoy your first pole fishing day!

A B O U T   T H I S   G U I D E

To help you locate a fishery, in the West Yorkshire area.
I have placed a float symbol with its location
number on the area map. See page 12

Each page contains details of a fishery,
with information on the following:

Ticket Price: Day ticket costs plus details on OAPs,
                         disabled and junior concessions.

Directions: Usually from the nearest city or town,
                         or from the closest motorway junction.

Description: A brief outline of what the fishery looks
                         like plus details on features such as
                         islands, depths and the best
                         places to fish.

Types of Fish: List of species present, many with
                         estimated weights.

Rules/Bans: The restrictions set by the fishery
                         on type of baits, hooks etc.

Number of Lakes: The number of waters available to
                         fish at the venue.

Facilities: What is available at each location
                         i.e. cafe.

Telephone: The number of the owner, angling
                         club secretary or match organiser.

Sat Nav: Post Codes for use on satellite
                         navigation systems.

Blood Knot

This knot can be used to join two lines together, start by overlapping the ends of the two lines.

Thread the end of your line through the eye of your hook.

Twist one end round the other line four times and pass it between the two lines.

Do the same with the other end of line, making sure the previous step does not come undone.

Before pulling tight wet the knot to lubricate this also make it hold better. Trim off the two ends.

Pull on the loose end to tighten. Trim the line.

Half Blood Knot

Used mainly for joining hook to line.

Pass the free end underneath the line and bring it back over the line to form a loop

Continue to loop the free end over the line about four times.

Pass the loose end between the eye of the hook and the first loop.

Double Overhand loop

This knot is used to create a loop at the end of a line. Also known as the surgeon's loop.

To begin, double the end of the line back against itself.

Tie an overhand knot in the doubled line.

The doubled end should then be tucked through the loop again.

Pull the knot as tight as possible and trim of the end.

Water Knot

This knot can also be known as the surgeon's knot. It is useful for joining a lighter hook line to your mainline

Hold the ends of the two lines alongside each other so that they overlap by about six inches.

Take hold of the two lines and make a wide loop.

Holding the two lines together. Pass the ends of the line through the loop four times.

Pull the lines tightly so that the loop makes a knot. Trim the two ends.

S P E C I E S / S Y M B O L S

Most commonly found in
the West Yorkshire area.

 BARBEL

 Camping

 BREAM

 Caravan Site

 CARP

 Drinks

 CHUB

 Disabled Access

 CRUCIAN

 Toilets

 IDE

 Food

 ORFE

 P Parking

 PERCH

 EEL

 PIKE

 GUDGEON

 ROACH

 33 Location of fishery on Map

 RUDD

To help you find the nearest
place to get tackle and bait,
turn to page 61
for a list of tackle shops
in West Yorkshire

 TENCH

TROUT

11

WEST YORKSHIRE VENUES

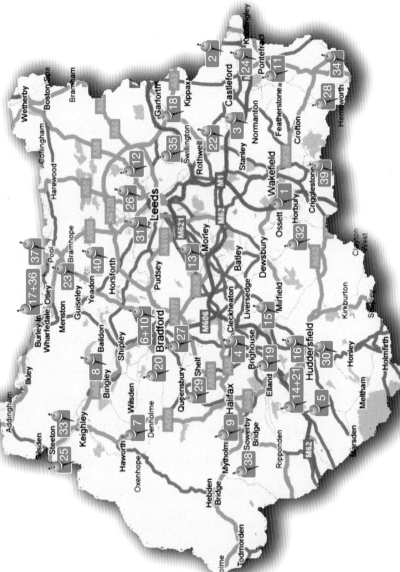

Benlee Lakes
Green Lane, Horbury, Wakefield.

Ticket Price: Day tickets £5.00 Concessions £4.00

Directions: From Wakefield take the A642 Horbury Road. Go under the M1 Motorway. After around a mile turn left into Mill Field Road. Take your second left onto Green Lane and continue to fishery.

Description: There are two square lakes to fish here at Benlee, both have 22 pegs on them. The depths is just under five feet, making this an ideal all year round fishery. There are no facilities except for secure parking.
The excellent platforms make for easy disabled access to most pegs. A good mixture of silver fish plus many good sized carp that reach double figures.

Types of Fish: The pond is very well stocked with roach, bream, skimmers, ide and carp.

Rules/Bans: No keepnets (unless in matches). Barbless hooks only.

Facilities: **Number of Lakes:** Two

Telephone: 01924 263500   **Sat Nav:** WF4 5DY

Birkin Fisheries

Haddlesey Road, Birkin.

Ticket Price: Day tickets £5.00

Directions: Come off the M62 at junction 33 and head North on the A162. Turn right at next roundabout (Sutton Lane). Go through two small villages until you reach Birkin. Turn left at the road junction. Haddlesey Road is on your right. Look for the fishery on your right.

Description: This fishery may be just over the border into North Yorkshire but is well worth a visit. It has two well stocked ponds with 58 pegs to chose from. You do tend to feel like you are fishing a river which makes a nice change from many fisheries. Both ponds have islands to fish up to, where many anglers were catching well. The average depth is around the six feet mark.

Types of Fish: Bream, tench, carp and plenty of silver fish .

Rules/Bans: No keepnets, barbless hooks only. Full set of rules are on a sign next to the lakes.

Facilities:

Telephone: 01977 673365

Sat Nav: WF11 9LS   **Number of Lakes:** Two

Birkwood Farm Fisheries
Altofts, Normanton, Wakefield.

Ticket Price: Day ticket £6.00.
Concessions and under 16's £5.00. After 1 pm £4.00
Tickets are transferable from lake to lake.

Directions: From the Wakefield / Leeds direction turn left off Aberford Road (A 642) towards Stanley Ferry. This is signposted Altofts and Normanton. Go past the Ship Pub, over the 2 bridges, up the hill and when you get to 2 white cottages turn left onto Birkwood Farm. Birkwood is 2 miles from the M62 (junction 30) and 3 miles from the M1 (junction 42 which is the M62 Junction).

Description: The Main Lake contains Carp to 25lbs, Roach, Rudd, Tench, Bream & Gudgeon. The lake fishes well all year round and has 28 pegs. The deepest part is 4 metres at the centre of the lake. Frog Hall Lake can accommodate 10 anglers. It is heavily stocked with Carp up to 27 lbs, Roach, Rudd, Perch and also has some Tench. Depth is around 3 metres in the middle. It is sheltered and in the far corner of the farm. Emily's Lake has 37 pegs and is heavily stocked with Carp. This has become a very popular day fishing and match fishing lake. Oscar's Lake is also heavily stocked with Carp but this lake is smaller with only 31 pegs. This stretch of the River Calder has hardly been fished before now. Stocked with Brown Trout , Rainbow Trout, Chub, Gudgeon, Roach, Rudd, Barbel.

Number of Lakes: Four lakes. One stretch of river.

Rules/Bans: Barbless hooks only, no keepnets except in matches.

Telephone: 01924 892251 **Facilities:**
Sat Nav: WF6 2JE

15

Brookfoot Lake
Elland Road, Brighouse.

Ticket Price: Adult £4 Concessions £2. Tickets should be bought in advance from Calder Angling Supplies or A.J Jewson fishing supplies.

Directions: Take the A6025 from Brighouse centre. After about 1 mile you will see the lake on your left hand side.

Description: Brookfoot is a three and a half acre lake that has been developed from an old gravel pit. It is a large open water with wonderful surroundings and wildlife. The lily beds, rushes and overhanging trees offer plenty of fish holding areas to target. The carp are an impressive size many reaching 26lbs. Plenty of large roach and a number of double figure bream. Three islands have recently been built, which breaks up the water and seem very popular to fish up to.

Types of Fish: Carp, bream, roach, perch, pike and chub.

Rules/Bans: Barbless hooks only. Keepnets are allowed but not for carp. No nuts allowed. No night fishing.

Facilities: P ♿

Number of Lakes: One

Sat Nav: HD6 2RN

Telephone: Brighouse Angling Association

Cellars Clough

Between Huddersfield and Oldham.

Ticket Price: Day ticket £5.00 for 1 or 2 rods.
Under 16's must be accompanied by an adult.

Directions: If travelling from Huddersfield, take the A62 to Oldham. Stay on this road and you will go through two small villages (Linthwaite and Slaithwaite). Once you have gone through both of these keep your eyes out for the garage on the left hand side of the road. About 1/2 a mile after the garage, you approach an S-Bend that curves first to the right. Before it curves back to the left there is a side road on your right hand side. This is the entrance to Cellars Clough.

Description: There are two ponds here, mill pond is the smaller one with bream to 7lbs and carp to 6lbs. The Main Lake has the larger carp in the 20's and some very big pike. This venue offers a very welcome atmosphere and is an ideal place to get away and relax.

Types of Fish: Mirror and common carp, bream, perch, roach, pike and the odd trout.

Rules/Bans: No carp, bream and pike to be kept in keepnets. Barbless hooks only. Full list of rules available on site.

Number of Lakes: Two   **Sat Nav:** Not available.

Facilities:

Telephone: 07833 552467

Chellow Dene
Allerton Road, Bradford.

Ticket Price: Tackle shop agents and fees, see on page 58

Directions: Follow signs for Allerton from Bradford Royal Infirmary. Just before roundabout and Reservoir pub, turn right opposite Olivers Gents barbers. Continue up Chellow Lane to the end and park near to the park gate house. Walk past first lake with Island, proceed up the steps to second fishery (club water) which can be found at the top.

Description: This water can be found in the middle reservoir of this 18th century water supply reservoir chain. Depths very from 6 to 32 feet, with the total area of the lake around 10 acres. This is a water with massive untapped potential, although several carp anglers have started to target this water, fishing dog biscuit and travelling light. In the summer the surface of the water can be seen to be almost covered with the roach and perch which are the main species. There are some massive carp in the water which can often be seen taking bread during the summer. The water holds a match record of 26lb of roach in a 4 hour evening match. This water was recently been stocked with over 3 thousand roach from a nearby park lake with many specimens over the pound mark. In the shallower water, pike can be found ranging from small jacks to some very large specimens. There are two entrances both entailing a walk in excess of 5 minutes. 2002's stocking program saw the introduction of 5,000 carp.

Facilities: None   **Number of Lakes:** One

Telephone:
01274 571175

Sat Nav: BD15 7AB
Information kindly supplied by
Bradford No1 Angling Association.

Doe Park Reservoir
Foster Park View, Denholme.

Ticket Price: Day tickets are available from tackle shops in the Keithley, Halifax and Bradford area. They are £5.00 and have to be bought prior to fishing.

Directions: From Halifax head towards Keighley on the A629. In Denholme turn right into Foster Park Road, which takes you onto Foster Park View. Follow this road down to the reservoir.

Description: Like many big waters the fish can be very spread out and locating them can be tricky. This reservoir is 20 acres in size and upto 50 feet deep in parts. Many anglers target the larger bream and tench with a feeder, using big chunks of meat as a hook bait. Plenty of small fish (roach, rudd and perch) can be caught on maggot. A few big carp are present along with chub.
Pike anglers love this water in the winter, with the record standing at just over 20lb.

Types of Fish: Carp, bream to 5lb, roach, perch, tench to nearly 6lb, rudd, pike 20lb. and chub.

Rules/Bans: No live baiting allowed.

Facilities: P **Sat Nav:** BD13 4BG **Number of Lakes:** One

Telephone: Bradford City Angling Association
01274 684906

7

Farview Fishing Lakes

Lee Lane, Bingley, Bradford.

Ticket Price: Adults, Mar 1st to Oct 31st - £6 per day.
After 4pm - £4. Nov 1st to Feb 29th - £5 per day.
O.A.P's - £5 per day. Children, 14 and under - £4 per day.

Directions: From Bingley take the B6265 (Bradford Rd)
heading towards Cottingley Bridge. After approximately 2
miles turn right onto the B6146 sign posted Allerton. Go
through Cottingley and turn right onto Lee Lane. The fishery
is a mile on your left.

Description: With two heavily stocked lakes spanning the
complex, there's something for everyone whether your into
carp, or the many other species stocked. Set in beautiful
Yorkshire countryside near Bradford the fishery provides a
peaceful and relaxing environment.

Types of Fish: Carp, chub, barbel, roach, tench, bream and
golden orfe.

Rules/Bans: Fishing is available from 7.00 am to sunset.
Fishing is with one rod, line and hook, pole only.
NO KEEPNETS ALLOWED (except in a pre-booked match).
No fish to be removed from site, anyone caught doing so
will be prosecuted. Anyone with litter in or around his or her
peg will be asked to leave. Barbless hooks.
Fishing is only allowed from designated platforms.
No fish to be held in cloths or towels. Natural baits only.
No braided hook lengths, dog or cat food or tiger nuts.

Number of Lakes: Two   **Facilities:**

Telephone: 01274 490444 / 07790 881323

Sat Nav: BD16 1UF

 8

Gratrix Lane Dam

Gratrix Lane, Sowerby Bridge.

Ticket Price: Tackle shop agents and fees, see on page 58

Directions: From Halifax take the A58 towards Sowerby Bridge. Just before the centre of Sowerby Bridge turn right into Gratrix Lane. The dam is 500 yards on the left.

Description: The water varies from 6 to 18 feet and is covered by heavy trees and foliage around the edges. Parking is near, safe and well open. The fishery is best described as an aquarium as all types of fish are present. Carp run to double figures and some large bream have been stocked. It is best to avoid setting up around the small inlet to fish, as later plumbing of the water may find depths to only 14 inch. It is misleading on first impression, but this water holds upto 100 carp all over 10lbs. There are chub well over 4lb, Ide over 2.5lb, and Bream to 6lb. Perch and small Roach can be caught with the float touching the dam wall at nearly all the pegs. Platforms have recently been erected at the water, making total pegs 12.

Types of Fish: Carp, bream, perch, roach, rudd, ide, gudgeon and chub.

Rules/Bans: Keepnets only in matches. Barbless hooks only.

Number of Lakes: One   **Sat Nav:** HX6 2DH

Facilities: P   &

Telephone: 01274 571175

Information kindly supplied by Bradford No1 Angling Association.

Harold Park Lake
Harold Park, Bradford.

Ticket Price: Tackle shop agents and fees, see on page 58

Directions: Travel down Manchester Road towards Brighouse. After the Drop Kick pub look for a petrol station on the right. Turn right before the petrol station. Take your third right (Park Road). Park in the car park.

Description: Harold Park can be found in a scenic recreational park, just minutes from Bradford City centre. It is one of the three lakes which make up the waters known as the Bradford Lakes. Depths vary from 3 to 18 feet with shallow water found around the island and old boat house. Access is straight from the car park and a watchful eye can be kept on both float and car. This is an excellent fishery for the disabled due to the easy access. Pole and feeder are productive methods, but the waggler with either maggot, bread or hemp count for many good nets. The park is often visited by locals who feed the ducks. It is the bread feed that over the last few years has had large carp revealing themselves and been targeted by the Carp anglers. Feeder fishing from the deep end (left of entry) has accounted for some nice specimen Bream.

Types of Fish: Carp, bream, perch and roach.

Rules/Bans: Keepnets only in matches. Barbless hooks only.

Number of Lakes: One   **Sat Nav:** BD12 0DL

Facilities: P ♿

Telephone: 01274 571175

Information kindly supplied by Bradford No1 Angling Association.

Hemsworth Water Park

Hoyle Mill Rd, Kinsley, Pontefract.

Ticket Price: Day tickets £3.00   Under 16's £1.50

Directions: Heading towards Wakefield on the A645. Take a left onto the B6428, and then take a left turn onto the B6273 towards Hemsworth. Turn left at the sign for the water park and the water can be found on the right hand side.

Description: There are around 60 pegs on the two lakes run by the county council. The first lake that you come to is in the shape of a figure eight and is the smallest of the two. It has an average depth of four feet and plenty of marginal reed beds to target near to the carpark. The second lake is known as "Windsurfer Lake", and the reason why is obvious. This lake has 35 pegs and is a little over 7 feet deep. This is a busy family venue with walkers and cyclists in abundance on nice days.

Types of Fish: The carp run to mid 20's, with tench caught at weights approaching 8lb. There are good shoals of bream to 4lb. There are some very big perch present, a few large eels and the remainder of the stock are Roach and gudgeon.

Rules/Bans: Barbless hooks only, no keepnets, no night fishing. Fishing from dawn until dusk.

Facilities: 🅿 ♿ ☕ 🚻

Number of Lakes: Two   **Sat Nav:** WF9 5JB

Telephone: 01977 617617

Highfields Fisheries

Highfields Farm, Long Lane, Barwick in Elmet.

Ticket Price: £5.00 from the farm or Bobs Tackle, Garforth.

Directions: From the M1, junction 47 head along the A642 into Garforth. Turn right after the railway bridge at the lights onto Barrowby Road and then immediately right again onto Barwick Road. Follow this road back over the M1 which becomes Long Lane and after the golf club at the top of the hill look out for Highfields Farm on your right where the fishery is sign posted.

Description: This lake has an average depth of just over 5 feet. It has an island which can be reached from one side with a pole and a feeder or bomb from the other. Fishing with chopped worm or meat seemed to be working for the larger fish. There are now 39 pegs, with a few clearly marked for disabled anglers, but unfortunately there are no toilets on site.

Types of Fish: The pond is very well stocked with roach, rudd, perch, chub, orfe, tench and carp into low double figures.

Rules/Bans: No keepnets (unless in matches). Barbless hooks only. Nets must be dipped. No ground bait. Under sixteen's must be accompanied by an adult. The syndicate generally have matches on a Sunday, so you should check beforehand to see if any pegs are available.

Facilities: P   ♿   **Number of Lakes:** One

Telephone: Bobs Tackle Shop,   **Sat Nav:** LS15 4EW
0113 2867112

Hillcrest Farm Fisheries

Scotchman Lane, Morley.

Ticket Price: £5.00 per day ticket. £3.00 after 12 noon which is collected on the bank side

Directions: Leave the M62 motorway at junction 27 and take the A650 heading towards Wakefield. When you come to a set of traffic lights with a big Toby Carvery on the left hand side, go straight on and follow the road for about 3/4 of a mile. When you reach another set traffic lights, turn right onto Scotchman Lane. follow the road again for about 3/4 of a mile and The Needless Pub is on your right hand side. The fishery is directly behind the pub.

Description: This small 3/4 of an acre pond is packed with good quality fish of various type. It has a small island in the middle which is the area to target for the carp which reach 10lbs. Pole fishing close in to the reed beds also works well especially for the tench that go up to 4lbs. The perch and roach come out for a single red maggot. Meat works for the carp and tench.

Types of Fish: Bream, perch, roach, tench, carp and ide.

Rules/Bans: Fishing dawn till dusk. No litter. Barbless hooks to be used at all times. No loose feeding of ground bait or nuts. Ground bait may be permitted in a small feeder. No keepnets allowed at any time. Landing nets must be dipped. No children under 16 without adult supervision.

Facilities:

♿ P

13

Number of Lakes: One

Sat Nav: LS27 0NX   **Telephone:** 01924 420405

Hill Top Reservoir
Slaithwaite, Huddersfield.

Ticket Price: Day tickets are available from tackle shops in advance of fishing. Day tickets £4.00 from Chris Roberts Tackle, HD1 3EB or Marsden Post Office.

Directions: Take the A62 from Huddersfield. Go through Slaithwaite town centre. You can access the water via a footpath on the corner of Bank gate and Royd Street.

Description: Another reservoir run by Slaithwaite and District Angling Club. This one is 11acres and is very deep, even at a rods length it is nearly ten feet. If you want carp the only way is to use an open feeder with meat on the hook. Pole fishing the margins will see plenty of good sized roach and perch coming out to a red maggot or worm. This is a renound pike fishery with record breaking sized catches.

Types of Fish: Bream, carp, roach, perch and pike.

Rules/Bans: Night fishing is allowed on this water.

Facilities: None

Telephone: 01484 656389

14

Sat Nav: HD7 5XE   **Number of Lakes:** One

Hopton Waters
Upper Hopton, Mirfield.

Ticket Price: Adult day ticket £5.00, OAP's £4.00.
Under 16's must be accompanied by an adult £2.50.

Directions: Hopton waters is situated off the B6118 at Kirkheaton. Its just 10 minutes from junction 25 of the M62 or 15 minutes from junction 38 of the M1.

Description: Hopton Waters is a family-run concern. It was purpose built 5 years ago to a high standard, featuring an island to incorporate quiet places for spawning and wildlife. The lake contains a good selection of healthy fish. All the species thrive in this clear based lake with larger weights being recorded with each passing year.

Types of Fish: Bream between 7 and 8lbs, tench to 7lbs. Common and mirror carp to over 26lbs. Orfe and golden orfe to 4lbs. Large stock of roach and perch.

Rules/Bans: Barbless hooks. No boilies. Ground bait in swim feeder only. No keepnets except in matches.

Number of Lakes: One

Facilities: Toilets, lakeside parking and disabled access.

Telephone: 01924 490357 Mob: 0771 263 0974

Sat Nav: Not available. Entrance off Highgate Lane

15

Huddersfield Broad
Huddersfield.

Ticket Price: £3 in advance from Mirfield Tackle, tel 01924 491275 or Chris Roberts Fishing Tackle, tel 01484545032

Directions: Approach Huddersfield on the A62 Leeds Road. Past the Zeneca factory and turn down Fieldhouse Lane, which leads to the canal near some playing fields on the right-hand side.

Description: There are three miles of quality fishing on this canal, controlled by Gas Club AC, providing great summer fishing. There is a wide variety of species present, including skimmers, bream, carp, crucian and tench. The canal is also home to the rare ide, which run to over 3lb. Most anglers rely on pole methods, but a Waggler can be useful when the canal is clear. Casters will sort a better quality of fish and chopped worm is a winning method here. Hotspots are the pegs immediately above and below the locks. Perch to 3.5lb have been caught on lobworm as well as roach to over 2lb on hemp, fished over casters.

Types of Fish: Bream, carp, crucian carp, tench, perch, roach and ide.

Facilities: None

Telephone: 01924 491275

16

Knotford Lagoon
Old Pool Road, Otley.

Ticket Price: Tackle shop agents and fees, see on page 58

Directions: Approaching Pool from Yeadon head into centre. Before the petrol station and bridge take left hand turn and continue on main road. Continue past Blue Barn animal feed store. Entry to fishery is further along main road before right hand bend. Parking is available all around the fishery.

Description: One of the most popular still waters owned by the club. This former gravel pit offers around 50 pegs. The fishery is the approximately 11.8 acres in size and depths range from 8 - 18 feet, with some smaller marginal depths. The key to successful angling on this water is to plumb carefully with pole or waggler, or when fishing further out to try and locate the numerous gravel bars. During the mid 1980's 700 carp were introduced to the fishery, which dominated angling for around a decade making this water a carp angling paradise. During 2003 a two year stocking plan was introduced consisting of over 3,500 lb tench, 10,000 Roach to 1lb, 5,000 skimmers to a 1lb and 480 bream to 6lb. In the past few years lots more bream, roach and tench have been stocked.

Types of Fish: Carp, bream, perch, roach, tench and pike.

Rules/Bans: Keepnets only in matches. Barbless hooks only.

Facilities: **Number of Lakes:** One

Telephone: 01274 571175

Sat Nav: LS21 1EQ   Information kindly supplied by Bradford No1 Angling Association.

Kippax Park Fishery

Brigshaw Lane, Kippex, Garforth.

Ticket Price: Day ticket £6.00. Leeds DASA members day ticket rate is £4.00

Directions: From the M1 junction 46take the A63. After Garforth turn right at the next junction onto the A656. Take the next right signposted Kippex. Follow this road to the centre of Kippex and turn left into Cross Hills. This road turns into Brigshaw Lane. You will find the fishery on the left at the bottom of the hill.

Description: Their are three lakes here at Kippex. Skylark and Lapwing are both coarse fishing lakes and Rainbow is for trout fishing only. Skylark is an ideal pleasure anglers lake, not too big with 20 pegs and some good sized carp present. Lapwing is more of a match lake with 27 pegs, a depth of 5 feet with a canal side feel. The long island is about 15 metres from the bank and is perfect to fish up to.

Types of Fish: Barbel, tench, ide, mirror and common carp, roach and trout.

Rules/Bans: No keepnets except in matches. Groundbait in pole cup or feeder only. Barbless hooks only.

Facilities: P ♿

Telephone: 0113 2482373 (Leeds DASA)

18

Sat Nav: LS25 7LD   **Number of Lakes:** Three

Kirklees Lagoon
Junction 25, M62.

Ticket Price: Tackle shop agents and fees, see on page 58

Directions: Take junction 25 off the M62, after Heartshead Moor Services. At the roundabout take first left towards Huddersfield. As the road drops down turn left into car park by Flower Van or park in laybys at the side of the road. Walk across field back towards the motorway to the Lagoon..

Description: A well attended and full featured lake made as a result of the M62 flyover spanning the River Calder. Depths range down to 16 feet in places. The lagoon is on the same water table as the River Calder and the water level can rise and fall. The water quality is excellent, but frequently the water becomes gin clear and fishing can be hard. Pegs are well established and easy to fish from. The main species sought at this venue are the carp and tench. Boillies are the most common bait. Although meat, worms and corn are all productive especially if fished close to features or behind the reed beds. It is well worth noting that the fish in this particular lake are not "domesticated" as those found in commercial fisheries and it is highly unlikely that any of the Carp or Tench 5lb upwards would be landed on present day pole equipment. There is also a very large head of Roach, which are caught on little and often feeding. There is also a large amount of perch plus the odd chub. Feeding on the shoals of fry and smaller fish are the usual pike. There are lots of jack pike which can become a nuisance, but easily targeted with a spinner or plug. The larger specimens 10Lb and above can be spotted from the banks hiding among the weed beds and are easily taken with sea or coarse dead baits.

Facilities: Carpark

Number of Lakes: One   **Telephone:** 01274 571175   19

Information kindly supplied by Bradford No1 Angling Association.

31

Leeds and Liverpool Canal
Silsden, near Bradford.

Ticket Price: Seniors £3. Juniors and Senior Citizens £1.50

Directions: Take the A629 to where it meats the junction of the A6034 follow this road to Silsden. Go over the canal and then take a left turn into Elliott Street. Follow this road down and you will come to a farm at the bottom. There is footbridge access to the far bank.

Description: This stretch of canal is renowned for its winter fishing for the roach and pike. It is only 15 metres wide. Reaching this shelve at the opposite side is quite easy. Depths are between 4 and 5 foot. Plenty of bream are caught here, with some reaching nearly 5lb. Roach are a good size to, getting close to 2lbs. You could get lucky and land one of the few large carp that have been seen close to the banks. Try meat or worm for them. Other fish present are perch, chub and tench.

Types of Fish: Bream, perch, roach, tench, carp and pike .

Rules/Bans: Full set of rules can be found on there website. (keighleyanglingclub.co.uk)

Facilities: None

Telephone: Keighley Angling Club

Sat Nav: BD20 0DE

Low Hills Pond
Plover Road, Lindley, Huddersfield.

Ticket Price: Day tickets £5.00 are available from Calder Angling Supplies or Jacksons Store on the main road in Lindley.

Directions: From Junction 23 off the M62, take the A640 (New Hay Road). When you reach Lindley look out for Plover Road on your left. Turn along Plover Road and you will find the lake about half a mile along on your left.

Description: This is a shallow man made pond with depths of only 2 feet in most areas, going to 4 feet in the centre. Great summer venue with plenty of lilies and other features to target. Most anglers were pole fishing with the exception of the one using a waggler. All were catching well on maggot or sweetcorn. You never know what your next fish might be on this heavily stocked small pond.

Types of Fish: Carp, roach, perch, bream, chub, gudgeon and barbel.

Rules/Bans: No groundbait allowed. No keepnets except in matches. Barbless hooks only.

Telephone: Not known   **Facilities:**

Sat Nav: HB3 3BZ   **Number of Lakes:** One

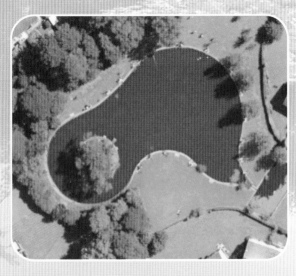

Lowther Lake
Allerton Bywater.

Ticket Price: Allerton Bywater AC. Season permits £16.00 OAP's £8.00 and under 16's £6.00. Permits from local tackle shops.

Directions: Take the A656 from Castleford. Turn left and go through Allerton Bywater heading for Great Preston. Turn left onto Nivevah Lane and park at the end of the lane.

Description: This 23 acre lake has two islands and has an average depth of around 8 feet. The main species caught are the large bream up to 10lbs and tench to 9lb. This is a member only lake so make sure you have your permit from the local tackle shop (The tackle shop, Kippax). There are plenty of roach to 2lb plus perch to 3lb. Great winter sport can be found fishing for the huge pike, some as big as 30lb. Try float fishing with maggot and caster, over a bed of hemp for the perch and roach.

Types of Fish: Bream, perch, roach, tench and pike and a few eels.

Rules/Bans: Keepnets only in matches. Barbless hooks only. Fishing is from dawn till dusk only.

Facilities: **Number of Lakes:** One

Telephone: 01977 559022

Sat Nav: WF10 2EW

Non Go Bye Farm
Otley Old Road, Cookridge, Leeds.

Ticket Price: Day tickets £5.00. After 4pm £3.00

Directions: Come off the A6120 ring road at the Weetwood roundabout. Take Otley Old Road and stay on this road as you drive through Cookridge. Follow the road till you reach a caravan site on your right. Turn next right into the farm.

Description: This all year round fishery has three ponds, two of which have islands that attract plenty of large carp especially to the corners. The average depth on all the ponds is between 5 and 6 feet. There has been a lot of work done on the paths around the water, along with some new pegs. This is making it an ideal fishery for the disabled angler. A great spot to take a novice angler as they are guaranteed a roach or perch every cast.

Types of Fish: Bream, carp, roach, perch, tench and chub.

Rules/Bans: Groundbait in feeder or pole cup only. No keepnets and only barbless hooks. All litter must be taken home.

Facilities: P 👤♿ 🚻

23

Telephone: 0113 2843968

Sat Nav: LS18 5HZ   **Number of Lakes:** Three

Pontefract Park Lake
Park Side, Pontefract Park, Pontefract.

Ticket Price: Adult £2.60. Junior £1.30
Adult twilight £1.95 Junior twilight £1.00

Directions: Come off the M62 at junction 32. Take the A639 (Park road) sign posted Pontefract. The lake is on your left just before Pontefract Racecourse.

Description: This is a small lake set in the grounds of a park. It has a concrete walkway all the way round making it ideal for the disabled angler. The park gets busy with walkers so don't leave your fishing pole over the path as a few have been stepped on. Try fishing with bread punch or sweetcorn, as most species will take this bait at only 10 metres from the edge. The perch reach a very reasonable size, around 2lb. This is a great lake for the novice angler and a cheap day ticket price. Good all year round fishery run by Wakefield council. Many anglers come for the pike in the winter months, these can reach 20lbs.

Types of Fish: Tench, bream, roach, perch, and pike to 20lb.

Rules/Bans: Barbless hooks only. No keepnets.

Facilities: Sat Nav: WF8 4RD

Telephone: 01977 723491   **Number of Lakes:** One

Raygill Fisheries.
Lothersdale, Keighley.

Ticket Price: £6 per day, £4 per half day (4hrs)
£4 per day concessions (OAP's & juniors under 16 yrs)
£10 per day for 2 rods.
Juniors MUST be accompanied by an adult (over 18 yrs).

Directions: If you are coming off the M65 go past
Matalan/KFC (on your right) and keep going straight on till
you come to the Morris Dancers Pub on your left. At the
next roundabout take 1st left signposted Lothersdale. Travel
on there about 3 miles (past the Black Lane Ends Pub) until
you go down a long dip and at the bottom you will see a
sign for us (turn Right). Raygill is tucked away in the small
picturesque village of Lothersdale. We are signposted from
3 miles away in each direction by tourist information signs.

Description: Large Coarse Lake (41 Pegs)
3.5 acres of fishing for roach, rudd, bream, perch, tench,
gudgeon, orfe & carp up to 30lbs. Many features and a
large variation in depth from 4ft to 14ft making interesting
sport on all sides of the lake. Small Coarse Lake (9 Pegs)
1 acre of fishing for carp up to 10lbs
Roach, bream, perch, tench, orfe, and gudgeon.

25

Rules/Bans: Keepnets only in matches. Barbless hooks only.
All anglers must dip nets before commencing to fish, unless
using a Raygill net. All litter, nylon and cigarette ends to be
taken home or placed in bins provided. All fishermen must
allow bailiffs to inspect their vehicles and fishing equipment
on request. Anglers under 16 years must be accompanied
by a person over 18 years old.

Number of Lakes: Two coarse lakes, two fly fishing lakes.

Facilities: ♿ 🅿 🚻 🍴   **Telephone:** 01535 632500
Sat Nav: BD20 8HH

Roundhay Park Lake
Roundhay, Leeds.

Ticket Price: Day tickets £3.00 from the cafe.

Directions: Roundhay Park is situated 3 miles north of Leeds City Centre off the A58 Wetherby Road at Oakwood. Alternatively, it is accessible from the A6120 Leeds Ring Road.

Description: This 15 acre lake is set in the middle of one of Leeds busiest parks The endless questions, such as have you caught much mate can be very frustrating. But if you find a quite spot the fishing especially for the bream is worth coming for. Their are a few big carp and pike present upto 20lbs. Plenty of silver fish to keep the kids happy.

Types of Fish: Bream, carp, roach, perch, tench, chub and pike.

Rules/Bans: Barbless hooks only, no keepnets, No night fishing.

Facilities:

Telephone: 0113 2425242 Leeds Council

26

Sat Nav: LS18 2LP   **Number of Lakes:** One

38

Royds Hall Dam
Woodside Road, Bradford.

Ticket Price: Tackle shop agents and fees, see on page 58

Directions: From the roundabout at the top of M606 take second left along the A6036 (Rooley Avenue), pass by Bradford Bulls Stadium. At next roundabout take the 3rd exit to Halifax A6036. Turn 4th left down Abb Scott Lane, then 2nd right onto Fenwick Drive. Take 2nd left onto Lingdale Road and park on the grass verge on your left. Walk thorough Walkers Entrance to field and down to reservoir. (type of walking - not suitable for wheel chairs but otherwise its a short level walk)

Description: This is a large reservoir with fishing on 3 banks. Depths vary from 6 to 30 feet and the reservoir offers around 30 to 40 pegs. It suffers badly in the worst weather as there is very little cover. The attendance figures on the banks prove that fish can be caught all year round even in the hardest of conditions. The dominant species are the huge shoals of roach, which if fed little and often can produce some large nets. Waggler is the main method for this species fished around 8 to 10 feet in depth with maggot sprayed over the top. The Bream are often caught when targeted with either a maggot or open feeder. Feeding well with groundbait is the key to a successful bream fishing day. In summer the cow drink area is favoured for Roach plus bonus Crucian Carp which have been stocked. In winter the wall incorporating the sluice is the most favoured area, or any area with the wind blowing from behind. There is also a 13 foot rod restriction on this water due to the overhead power lines.

Types of Fish: Carp, bream, perch, roach, and crucian carp.

Rules/Bans: Keepnets only in matches. Barbless hooks only.

Facilities: P   **Number of Lakes:** One

Telephone: 01274 571175

Sat Nav: BD12 0TX   Information kindly supplied by Bradford No1 Angling Association.

Sally Walsh's Dam
Hoyle Mill Rd, Hemsworth.

Ticket Price: Coarse fishing day ticket £3.00, Concessions £1.50. Carp fishing £7.00. 24hr £14.00

Directions:

Description: This mixed coarse fishery has plenty for every angler, especially for the carp fisherman, with some of the largest fish in South Yorkshire recorded in this dam. The water is surrounded by trees and has lots of reed beds to target close to the bank

Types of Fish: Common carp, mirror carp, bream, tench, roach, and perch.

Rules/Bans: Keepnets to be used only during matches. Barbless hooks only. No nuts.

Number of Lakes: One

Facilities:

28

Telephone: 01226 203090   **Sat Nav:** WF9 5JB

Shelf Dam
Cock Hill Lane, Shelf.

Ticket Price: Tackle shop agents and fees, see on page 58

Description: A small well established lake. Depths vary from 6 to 22 feet. Care should be taken on the first visit when staking out nets or placing rods rests as the sides of the dam drop vertically to

Directions:

depths of 16 feet. The main species targeted are the roach. There is a massive head of these in the dam with specimens around the 1lb mark. Perch are also common to around 1lb. Bream and skimmers have been recently stocked plus some established large bream to the 6lb mark are present. There are also around 50 carp to 20lb. Pole fished down the margin is best method or waggler/stick fished with meat or corn catches the carp and tench. Roach can be caught on light tackle in the edge on the bottom on pinkie or bread punch. All species can be caught up in the water with bait sprayed and fished on the drop. Last years best Carp was over 19lb and best noted bag was 36lb of Roach and Bream.

Facilities: **Number of Lakes:** One

Rules/Bans: Barbless hooks only.

Telephone:
01274 571175

Information kindly supplied by
Bradford No1 Angling Association.

Sparth Reservoir
Marsden, Huddersfield.

Ticket Price: Day tickets are available from tackle shops in advance of fishing. Day tickets £4.00 from Chris Roberts Tackle, HD1 3EB or Marsden Post Office.

Directions: Take the A62 Manchester Road from Slaithwaite. Turn right just before the reservoir and follow the road round. Turn into Park Gate Road and follow to the end, where you will find the carpark on the left.

Description: This seven acre water is run by Slaithwaite and District Angling Club. Most anglers were using a groundbait feeder while targeting the large head of bream that are present, many reaching 7lb. The odd pole fishermen were pulling out perch and roach on bread punch and maggot. The water drops to twenty feet in areas but does seem to be snag free. Great pike fishing in winter, some reaching 20lb.

Types of Fish: A few carp, bream to 7lb, roach, perch, pike 20lb.

Rules/Bans: Fishing dawn till dusk. Barbless hooks only.

Facilities: **Sat Nav:** Not available

Telephone: 01484 656389   **Number of Lakes:** One

Spring End Farm.
Geldard Road, Leeds.

Ticket Price: £5.00. Concessions £3.00. After 4pm £2.50.

Directions: The water is situated on the outskirts of Leeds on the A62 Geldard Road. Come off the M621 at Junction 1 and head back under the motorway towards Pudsey. At the first set of traffic lights you need to turn left. Follow the road till you see some portakabins. This is where you need to turn right which will take you up a hill. You will see the pond behind some trees. The car park is on your right.

Description: This small pond is quite shallow and easy to fish, making it an ideal pond for youngsters and beginners. Take maggots and sweetcorn and you can catch roach and perch all day long. Try fishing up to the three islands if you want the larger carp that are present.

Types of Fish: There are a good head of carp, chub, perch, roach, golden orfe and tench.

Rules/Bans: No keep nets. You must have a landing net and it must be dipped before fishing. Barbless hooks only. No ground bait. No upsetting the sheep!

Facilities: Porta- loo on site.

Number of Lakes: One

Telephone: 0794 1736938   **Sat Nav:** LS27 7NG

31

Spring Valley Waters
Green Lane, Horbury.

Ticket Price: Day ticket £6.00. After 4pm £3.00

Directions: Take the A642 from Wakefield and head towards Huddersfield. When you reach Horbury turn right into Daw Lane. At the T junction turn right and then first left onto Green Lane. Follow the lane to the end and go under the motorway. The water is on your right.

Description: Set next to the M1 motorway, this water is a little on the noisy side. But don't let that put you off, the fishing is excellent, especially if its carp your wanting. Many locals come here in the evening, where its reported they can catch well over 100lbs in 3 hours. If you would rather target the tench (some as large as 8lb) try sweetcorn or soft hookable pellets with a small amount of groundbait. There are not many species missing from this water. Here's a list of the ones I know about. Carp, some too 21lbs, tench to 8lbs, bream to 6lbs, chub to nearly 4lbs, ide, eel, roach, rudd, barbel and perch.

Rules/Bans: Barbless hooks only, no boilies, no keepnets. Fishing is dawn to dusk,

Facilities: **Sat Nav:** WF4 5DY

Telephone: Not known   **Number of Lakes:** Two

Stake Hill Fishery
Heights Lane, Silsden, Keighley.

Ticket Price: Day tickets £6.00. Under 16's and OAP's £4.00. £4.00 after 4pm. Tickets on the bank.

Directions: Take the A660 from Leeds, sign posted Otley. Stay on the A660 until you reach a roundabout. Take the A65 in the direction of Ilkley. Drive though Ilkley until you reach a roundabout 3 miles after Ilkley. Take the first exit toward Silsden. Turn right onto Cringles Lane.
Keep going on this road, when you reach a crossroad, go straight over onto Heights Lane. Look for the fishery sign on your right.

Description: This is a beautiful fishery set in the country side overlooking the Aire Valley. This small twelve peg pond is stuffed with various species of fish. This is a young pond, opened in 2007, so don't expect large double figure carp, but they are growing nicely. Most anglers were pole fishing at about ten metres and catching on sweetcorn, maggot and luncheon meat.

Types of Fish: Bream, carp, roach, tench, and rudd.

Rules/Bans: No keepnets, Barbless hooks only.
Fishing from dawn till dusk.

Facilities: P ♿ 🚻

33

Telephone: 01535 653518 or 07813 661984

Sat Nav: BD20 9HW   **Number of Lakes:** One

Stubbs Hall Lakes
Stubbs Hall Farm, Hampole.

Ticket Price: Day tickets are £5.00

Directions: Leave the A1 at the Redhouse junction, and join the A638 heading to Wakefield. In about two miles you should see a signpost for the fishery on your left.

Description: This fishery has 2 lakes, one is reserved for fly fishing the other is for coarse fishing. This clean, well maintained site has good access all round the lakes, ideal for the disabled angler. Both lakes are about three acres in size but beware they are very exposed to the wind. There are 46 good pegs and two islands in the coarse lake.

Types of Fish: I am told there are as many as six different types of carp in the coarse lake. The smaller carp are between 3 and 6lb, the largest one was recorded at 34lb. There are also some good sized tench and chub. Roach, bream and perch make up the remaining species.

Rules/Bans: Keepnets, only in matches. Barbless hooks only. All litter must be removed from site.

Number of Lakes: Two

Sat Nav: DN6 7EZ

Facilities: 🚻 🅿 ♿   Take away food service available
01977 608100

Telephone: 07771 523128

34

Swillington Park
Swillington, Leeds.

Ticket Price: Day ticket £6.00 Concessions £5.00 (under 16's must be accompanied by an adult). Specimen Lake £10.00

Directions: Swillington Park is easily accessible from Wakefield Road (A642). It is only 5 miles out of Leeds, and minutes from junction 46 on the M1.

Description: There are four lakes to try at Swillington Park. Lake 1, The Match Lake has plenty of carp between 2lbs and 10lbs. Lake 2, Traditional Course Lake has tench and bream to 10lbs. Lake 3, Course and Match Lake contains roach, rudd, tench, perch and some large carp to 20lb. Lake 4, Big Carp Lake, has over 100 large carp in the 20s and is more suited to the dedicated carp angler.

Rules/Bans: Barbless hooks only, no keepnets.

Number of Lakes: Four, plus one under construction.

Facilities:

Telephone: 0113 2869129 mob 07970 037475
            Website: www.ratherbefishing.co.uk

Sat Nav: LS26 8QA

Toms Pond
Otley.

Ticket Price: Day ticket £5.00 (2 rods)
£1.00 for use of a keepnet.

Directions: From Otley town centre, take the A659 road.
After a mile turn right into East Busk Lane. Follow the lane
to the bottom, continue on the farm track and turn into the
farm at the very end.

Description: If you are wanting larger carp, try the first of the
two ponds, nearest the carpark. These carp are best
caught close up to the island using luncheon meat or
sweetcorn on the bottom. Later in the day floating baits
also work very well. Plenty of silver fish can come out to
red maggot or bread punch. There are plenty of reeds and
rushes that can be targeted from most pegs. The average
depth on both ponds is around three feet, but there are the
odd holes that drop to six feet.

Types of Fish: Carp, bream, tench, roach and chub.

36

Rules/Bans: Groundbait in feeders and pole cups only, no
litter. Barbless hooks.

Facilities: P   **Sat Nav:** LS21 1DU   **Number of Lakes:** Two

Telephone: 01943 461441 or 01943 462770

Weeton Lake
Avon Lodge, Huby, Leeds.

Ticket Price: Day tickets £6.00 for one rod.

Directions: From Leeds take the A658, main road to Harrogate. After 3 miles you will enter the village of Huby. Turn right into Weeton Lane. The lake is behind the last house before the bridge.

Description: This small pond of only a quarter of an acre and is set in the owners back garden. A large amount of common ghost and mirror carp have been stocked in this pond which are giving great entertainment as well as large nets of between 40 - 50lbs. Most swims can be reached with a pole and that's what most people were fishing with. Luncheon meat and soft hookable pellets are the preferred baits. Should you get bored with catching carp! You could try the trusty red maggot for the roach and rudd. Plenty of chub, bream and tench present as well.

Types of Fish: Carp, bream, roach, tench, rudd and chub.

Rules/Bans: Open 8.30am until dusk. Barbless hooks only, no microbarbs - maximum hook size 10. Only one rod to be used at any time. Please keep to permanent pegs. Mini pellets only - no nuts, boilies, dead/live baiting, method feeders or braid hook lengths. Please remove all litter and discarded fishing tackle bait

Facilities: **Sat Nav:** LS17 0HE   37

Telephone: 01423 734062   **Number of Lakes:** One

49

Willow Hall Dam
Steps Lane, Sowerby Bridge.

Ticket Price: Tackle shop agents and fees, see on page 58

Directions:

Description: A one and half acre well established lake.

Depths vary from around 6 to 22 feet, and most pegs on the nearside are well dug and maintained. The main species present are Roach and Perch and can be caught from any peg, high in the water in summer and at around 10 - 16ft in the winter. Most pegs can find a depth of 16 feet deep at around 8 meters from the bank. Skimmers and the occasional large bream can be caught on the bottom, with Bream specimens reaching around the 5lb mark. There are some very large tench in this lake to 5lb plus, and can be caught from the far bank in the pegs near the garages. Also some large common carp are stocked to around 15lb with an odd big fish to around the 20lb mark. Meat is the best bait for the Tench and Carp to avoid smaller fish. Eels are common under any overhanging bushes or near the reeds to worm or white maggot.

Types of Fish: Roach, perch, tench, carp, bream and eels.

Facilities: P   ♿   **Number of Lakes:** One

Telephone: 01274 571175   **Sat Nav:** HX6 2JH

38

Information kindly supplied by Bradford No1 Angling Association.

Wintersett Reservoir

Wintersett, Wakefield.

Ticket Price: Membership: Adults £42. Juniors £11. 16 to 18 yrs old £18. Senior Citizens £18.

Directions: From Barnsley take the A61 north to Staincross. Turn right onto the B6428, go through Royston, then on to Ryhill. Turn left then left again towards Cold Hiendley, then right to Wintersett.

Description: Wintersett reservoir is part of a complex of three lakes, Botany Lake and Cold Hiendley Reservoir make up the other two. All are run by Leeds & District Amalgamated Society of Anglers. Originally built as a top up for the Aire and Calder Navigation this 93 acre water is over twenty feet deep in parts. Good fishing can be had on the half moon bank, where plenty of bream can be caught, some as big as 9lb. There are also roach and perch to a resonable size. You will need 8lb line, a hair rig and a big chunk of luncheon meat for the carp.

Types of Fish: Carp, bream, roach, tench, perch, chub, pike and eels.

Rules/Bans: No hemp or tares. No night fishing. Check livebait and keepnet rules.

Facilities: **Sat Nav:** WF4 2DS

Number of Lakes: Three

Telephone: Leeds DASA. 0113 2482373

Yeadon Tarn

Cemetery Road, Yeadon, Leeds.

Ticket Price: Adult £4 Child £2, Tickets should be bought in advance from Headingley Angling Centre.

Directions: Take the A658 out of Leeds. Turn left onto High Street. Take your third right just after Club Row. This is Cemetery Road and the lake and carpark are on your right.

Description: The lake covers three and a half acres of a busy park. There can be problems with the amount of traffic behind your peg, so don't leave your pole over the path or a cyclist may ride over it. Don't let this and the sail boats put you off as there are plenty of fish in the lake. There is a good head of both carp and bream with most around 5lbs. Roach and perch can be caught all day long on maggot or bread punch.

Types of Fish: Carp, bream, roach, perch and a few tench

Rules/Bans: Barbless hooks only, no keepnets, no night fishing. Fishing from dawn until dusk.

Facilities:  Sat Nav: LS19 7UR

Number of Lakes: One   **Telephone:** 0113 2559530

Keep a record of all your fishing trips with

Log-it

Venue:		Address:			Date:
Peg No:	Start Time:		End Time:	Weather Conditions:	

Species	Weight	Method	Rig set up	Ground Bait	Hook Bait	Time

Venue:		Address:			Date:
Peg No:	Start Time:	End Time:		Weather Conditions:	

Species	Weight	Method	Rig set up	Ground Bait	Hook Bait	Time

Venue:		Address:			Date:
Peg No:	Start Time:		End Time:	Weather Conditions:	

Species	Weight	Method	Rig set up	Ground Bait	Hook Bait	Time

Bradford No1 Angling Association
Membership Fees & Agents

Subscriptions:

Juniors	(under 17 years old)	£14
Ladies		£16
Veteran	(over 65 years old)	£16
Full "Senior (male)"	(over 17 years old)	£36
Joining Fee	(not Juniors)	£20
Second rod permit	(allows 2nd rod on all venues)	£14
Privilege tickets	(allows a guest with full adult)	£3
Night Fishing	(Allows night fishing on either Knotford or Kirkless lagoons)	£50

Membership Permits are available from the following shops:

A.J.Jewsons Ltd
28 Horton Street
Halifax
tel 01422 354146

Angling and Country Sports.
36 Cross green
Pool Road.
Otley
tel 01943 462770

Chris Roberts Tackle
22 Chapel Hill
Huddersfield
tel 01484 545032

Castleford Angling Supplies
143 Lower Oxford St
Castleford
tel 01977 550465

Eccleshill Angling
13 Stoney Lane
Eccleshill
Bradford
tel 01274 627989

Gee Tee
19A Briggate,
Silsden,
tel. 01535 - 655555

Grahams Fishing Tackle
87 Crossbank Rd
Batley
tel 01924 442040

K.L. Tackle
127 North Street
Keighley
tel 01535 667574

Kirkgate Anglers
95 Kirkgate
Leeds
tel 0113 234 4880
www.tackle2u.com

Leeds Angling Centre
14 Branch Road.
Armley
tel 0113 263 9333

Nigel Hirst
727Huddersfield Road
Ravensthorpe
Dewsbury
tel 01924 491275

Outwood Angling
557-559 Leeds Road
Outwood
Wakefield
tel 01924 835443

Tackle2U.com
905 Manchester Road
Bradford
tel 01274 729570

Wibsey Angling
208 High Street
Wibsey
Bradford
tel 01274 604542

F I S H I N G T E R M S

Here is a list of the words most commonly used. This will help anglers new to the sport to understand fishing terms used by other anglers.

BALE ARM: A revolving arm on a fixed spool reel which winds line onto the spool.

BAGGING UP: A term used when an angler is catching really well, or to describe a venue that is fishing well.

BAIT BANDS: These are small rubber bands. They are aimed at securing difficult to hook baits to the hook. They come in various sizes to accommodate the size of the bait.

BAITING NEEDLE: These pull the hair loop through the bait. They have a mechanism for attaching to the loop whether it is like a small hook, or a pivot that hooks over the loop. The needle is then drawn back through the bait taking the loop and hair with it.

BARBLESS: A type of hook without sharp barbs to help retain bait and fish. Barbed hooks are banned from most fisheries.

BIN LIDS: A slang term for large bream.

BITE ALARMS: These are electronic sensors that detect the movement of line caused by the fish. They usually have an audible alarm or light to alert the angler.

BIVIES: These are domed tents with an opening at the front providing a shelter from the elements.

BOILIES: These are generally hard balls of bait that are primarily designed as a carp bait.

BREAD PUNCH: A bread punch has a circular 'punch' at the end which is pushed down onto a slice of bread and cuts a small piece out which is placed on the hook. There are many different sizes of punches for different hook sizes.

BREAKING STRAIN: The amount of pressure a line will take before snapping.

BUMPED OFF: This term is used by pole anglers, whereby through the use of heavy tactics the fish once hooked is bumped off. This happens when the fish is not big enough to expand the elastic fully.

CASTERS: The chrysalis form of a maggot.

DEADBAITING: The use of dead fish for catching predatory fish such pike, perch, and eels.

DISGORGER: A long device to help remove the hook from a fish's mouth. Always have one with you.

FOUL HOOKED: A fish that has been hooked anywhere else on the body apart from the mouth.

GROUNDBAIT: A dry mixture intended to be thrown into the water to attract fish. Usually consists of bread crumb, crushed biscuit, crushed hemp or other ingredients.

HAIR RIG: A hair rig is generally a piece of line that extends beyond the point of the shank of the hook. On the end of the length of line is a small loop.

HOOKLENGTH: A short length of line, of lesser breaking strength than the mainline, to which the hook is tied. It is used to make it less likely to be detected by the fish. It also ensures that if the line is snapped by a fish, the angler would not then lose the float / swim feeder / leger and all the other shot

LEGERING: Bait held on the bottom by means of a weight or feeder.

LOOSEFEED: Small offerings of loose bait, such as maggots or sweetcorn, which are thrown into the water to keep the fish interested in the area you are fishing.

LINE BITES: False indications of bites usually caused by fish brushing against the line.

LURES: Artificial fish, used to tempt predators such as pike and zander.

MARGIN: This is an area nearest the bank, that has a shallower depth than that of the main water.

MATCH FISHING: A competitive form of coarse fishing which involves people drawing out a random peg (a place to fish), and then trying to catch as many fish as possible within the allotted time. Usually the winner will be the one with the greatest weight of fish caught.

PEG: A peg is a pre defined fishing area. Venues are split up into evenly spaced fishing zones which are often marked with a wooden peg or marker.

PINKIES: The larvae of the green bottle fly. Small, very lively and great as a loosefeed on stillwaters and canals or as a hookbait for smaller fish.

PLUMMET: A device used for determining the depth of the water in which you are fishing.

POLE: A pole is constructed from very advanced carbon combinations and comes in various sizes, weight and prices.

POLE RIG: These are lengths of line that have the float, weights and a hook attached.

QUIVER TIP: A special type of rod used to detect bites when ledgering. It has a sensitive tip that curves over when the angler has a bite. Quiver tips vary in strength and stiffness which can be changed according to the weather conditions.

SNAGS: Features in your swim that are likely to cause you problems They can also be fish holding features such as lilies, overhanging trees, sunken branches. A place to avoid once a fish is hooked.

SPADE END HOOKS: Spade end hooks have an up-turned flattened piece of metal instead of an eye to which to tie the fishing line.

SPECIMEN: A term given to any fish that is a particularly good size for its species.

STRIKE: To respond to the taking of the bait by pulling the rod in an upwards or sideways motion to hook the fish.

SWIM: The area of water where you are fishing.

Tackle: A term used to refer to any fishing equipment (photo tackle)

TEST CURVE: The test curve is the time and weight needed to make the tip bend 90 degrees from the rod butt. Each rod has a test curve with those being used for specimen fish such as carp having a greater test curve than a general coarse rod.

TROTTING: Allowing a float to travel at the speed of the current.

WHIP: This is a scaled down version of a pole.

West Yorkshire Tackle Shops

Addlees, 30 High Street, Upton, Pontefract.	01977 658803
Angling & Country Sports, 36 Cross Green, Otley.	01943 462770
Bob-Co Tackle, 11 Cherry Row, Mabgate, Leeds.	0113 2461475
Bob's Tackle Shop, 1a Chapel lane, Garforth, Leeds.	0113 2867112
Calder Anglers Supplies, 39a Rastrick Common, Brighouse.	01484 711063
Castleford Angling, 143 Lower Oxford Street, Castleford.	01977 550465
Catch Fishing Supplies, Ackroyd Street, Morley, Leeds.	0113 2532525
Chris Roberts Fishing Tackle, 22 Chapel Hill, Huddersfield.	01484 545032
E&J Fishing Tackle, 20 Middleton Park Road, Leeds.	0113 2760034
Eric's Angling Centre, 401, Selby Rd, Whitkirk, Leeds.	0113 2646883
Featherstone Angling Centre, 15-17 Station Lane, Featherstone	01977 602822
Fred Alexanders Fishing Tackle, 3 The Springs, Wakefield.	01924 373820
Gee Tee (Angling Supplies), 13 Briggate, Silsden, Keighley.	01535 655555
Graham's Fishing Tackle, 57 Cross Bank Road, Batley.	01924 442040
Guisley Angling Centre, 84 Otley Road, Guisley.	01943 879938
Hemsworth Angling Centre, 83 Kirby Road, Hemsworth.	01977 614222
Nigel Hirst Fishing Tackle, 727 Huddersfield Road, Dewsbury.	01924 491275
Holme Valley Sports, 76 Huddersfield Road, Holmfirth.	01484 684128
Hunslet Angling Centre, 321 Hunslet Road, Leeds.	0113 2706949
A.J Jewson, 28 Horton Street, Halifax.	01422 354146
Kerr's Angling Centre, 26 Junction Lane, Ossett. WF5 0HA	**01924 263500**
Kirkgate Anglers, 95 Kirkgate, Leeds.	0113 2434880
www.tackle2u.com, 27 Racca Green, Knottingley.	01977 607706
Lathkill, 19a King Cross Street, Halifax.	01422 354444
Leeds Angling Centre, 14 Branch Road, Armley, Leeds.	0113 2639333
Lower Wharfe Angling Centre, 236 High Street, Wetherby.	01937 844260
N Marsh, 292 Upper Town Street, Bramley, Leeds.	0113 2649530
Morley Match Anglers, 47a Queen Street, Morley, Leeds.	0113 2537688
Mutleys Tackle & Bait, 74 Town Street, Horsforth, Leeds.	0113 258 2642
Outwood Angling Centre, 557-559 Leeds Road, Wakefield.	01924 835443
Premier Angling Centre, 64 Station Lane, Featherstone.	01977 600100
Pudsey Angling Supplies, Richardshaw Lane, Pudsey.	0113 2557900
Richmonds, 71 Park Road, Bradford.	01274 721042
JT Rogers, 12 Barwick Road, Crossgates, Leeds.	0113 2641195
S&B Angling Supplies, Pontefract Road, Crofton.	01924 864116
Tackle Box, 22 Cross Hills, Kippax, Leeds.	0113 2861435
Tipstrike, 4 Butt Hill, Kippax, Leeds.	0113 2873092
Upton Angling Centre, 30 High Street, Upton.	01977 658803
Westgate Anglers, 63 Westgate, Bradford.	01274 729570
West Park Angling, 572 Thornton Road, Bradford.	01274 548289
Wibsey Angling Centre, 208 High Street, Wibsey, Bradford.	01274 604542
Woodside Fishing Tackle, 1 Spibey Lane, Rothwell, Leeds.	0113 2828176

I N D E X

If you know of a fishery that is not included in this guide or you want to update an existing venue. Please fill in the form below.

Fishery Name

Fishery Address

Post code

Contact Name

Telephone No

| Adult Day Ticket Price | £ | concession OAP'S | £ |

Fish species and approximate weights

Brief Description

Rules / Bans

Facilities

Number of Lakes

Please e-mail or post a colour photo for inclusion in the next publication.

Please return this form to:
Arc Publishing
166 Knowle Lane,
Bents Green,
Sheffield S11 9SJ.

chris_keeling@tiscali.co.uk

New Fishery ☐

Update to Fishery ☐

New Fishery / Fishery Update Form

NOTES